Meet IC

Gill Cornfield

©Text, Photographs and Illustrations, Gillian A. Cornfield 2006

Foreword Endorsement

"The lyrics of my song, 'Read my name', sum up the achievements of the children who have made a contribution to this book".

With best wishes,
Chris de Burgh

Chris De Burgh

Dedication

This book is dedicated to the person who encouraged me to write about TC, and in doing so, launched a project.

For my daughter, Louise,

With Love

Acknowledgements

Special thanks to Chris De Burgh for allowing me to quote from his song, "Read my Name". His belief in this project by endorsing the book personally means so much to me, the children and the schools.

My grateful thanks to Denise Robertson, writer and presenter on ITV's This Morning, for reading the first draft of this book and giving me invaluable professional editorial advice.

Thank you to all the people who have made a contribution towards printing costs and wish to remain anonymous.

My thanks to Julian for his support as my partner, printing the drafts for use in the schools, and as a husband for being my rock.

To Paul many thanks for his confidence in me, his spontaneity and kindness in allowing me to work with the children, who laid the foundation stones for this book.

To Graham, my thanks for his skilful artwork, his endless patience and for overseeing the production of the book.

To Bishops Printers Ltd., for taking such a personal interest in this project.

Thank you to all the Bournemouth business and professional people who have supported us.

To the Children and Schools

A huge thank you to St. Thomas Garnet's School and Stourfield Junior School, with additional help from Year 1 Stourfield Infants School.

My thanks to the head-teachers, teachers and parents for their belief in this book and their unstinting support.

To the children: This is not an ordinary book. It is unique, because all of you (aged 6 – 11 years) who listened to the story for the first time, connected with TC (through the photographs) because he is real. You wanted to draw and edit, giving me vital feedback. In doing so, we became a team, creating a book, which developed a life of its own. You breathed energy into this project, and every single one of you has given your best. The words of Chris De Burgh's song, "Read my Name" sum up everything we are trying to achieve – children making a difference to the world. Thank you to the editors, and enjoy reading your name in TC's outline opposite.

To the individual illustrators, you have been tremendous, bringing my ideas to life in your own special way. I know that all children will enjoy looking at your wonderful drawings. Thank you so much, in alphabetical order, to:

Alexander	Ersan Beskardes	Kyle Morrell
Benji	Amber Cook	Ryan Morrell
Charlie	Maria Degan	Rebecca Murphy
Hannah	Robert Degan	Christopher Nichols
Henry	Nadia Foy	Jordan Norris
Jacob	Izzy Freeman	Amber Porter
Jake	Paeris Giles	Christie Quinn
Jeremy	Danny Grant	Haydon Ricketts
Lewis	Alexandra Hibberd	Catherine Shelton
Luther	Rory Lindsay	Harriett Wragg
Oliver	Amy Mack-Nava	
Ross		

Thanks also to all the Year 3 children at Stourfield Junior School for their imaginative and original "stick cats".

Read my name

Cameron Sam
Jordan William
Brandon Marlee
Paige Calum Ross
Abi James Boston
Jordan Abbie Charlie
Bradley Alix Ellisia
Kieron Mason Stephen
Ellena Anastasia Ted
Paris Joshua Jessica
Cameron Bertie Dylan Eva
Georgia Bethan Isabel Ben
Thomas Koto Matthew Harry
Emile Joseph Ziqiao Eoghan
Kieran Harry Alex Chloe Jack
Bethany Jack Matthew Emma
Rebecca Sophie Elliott Jordan
Bethany Sophie Georgia Megan Jack
Jarad Joel Jemma Sonny Toni
Benjiman Mark Benjamin Lewis
Lauren Kayleigh Nikol Olivia
Ruby Laura Poppy Jake Nadia
Luke Jennifer Samuel Lili Mae
Jack Conner Megan Jack Aisling
Laura Angel Amber-Rose Jessica
Alisha Callum Thomas Yasmin
Harry Karla Lydia Daniel
Quentin Sian Jack Reece
Brady Emma Daisy Phoebe
Samara Eden Anna Jolon Olivia
Catherine Daniel Jake Scott
Jasmin Emily Lamara Luke

> "For every child that has been born, there is a chance to shine...
> With all I've got, I've taken part, I've made a difference to the world.
> I have been here – just read my name!"

"Read my name" lyrics, written by Chris De Burgh appear courtesy of the Publisher Hornall Brothers Music Ltd

Meet TC

Page 12   TC goes exploring

Page 30   Party with TC

Hello, Everyone. I'm up here, on my favourite green blanket. Children-peoples, it's lovely to see you again.

For those of you who haven't met me before, my name is TC. As you can see, I am 'Totally Cool', but you can find out how I got my name at the end of the book.

I am a real cat, and I live in Dorset with my family, Mum, Dad and Lou.

I live in the Utility Room (where my people wash and dry their clothes). I call it my Tilly Room.

I have one really good mate, Chris Mouse, who lives on the pipe behind the washing machine. He broke into my Tilly room some time ago. At first, I chased him, but we soon became great chums, and I can't imagine life without him. In fact, I think I can hear him, now!

"Chris, is that you?"

"Yes, TC."

"Come and meet the children-peoples. This is the first time some of them have met us, not all of them read the first book."

"You mean there are more children-peoples, TC, I've come over all shy."

"No you haven't, Chris. Say, 'Hello' properly."

"Hello properly."

"Chris, just say 'Hello' and stop messing around."

By the way, everyone, I should say 'Children-peoples' is my special name for you. It's TC talk. That means it's my special cat name for you all.

"TC, I'm ready now. Hello to all you children-peoples in the country I haven't met before. I'm Chris Mouse, TC's best friend in the whole world."

"I see you've lost your shyness, Chris, but that's enough, because I'm going to start my story."

Now, I want you to sit back and chill, because I'm going to tell you about an adventure I had when I was a kitten-baby, and it really happened. At that time, I was so tiny I could sit in the palm of Dad's hand.

For this part of the book, I have a stunt double. Here he is, a little toy kitten belonging to Lou. Now turn the page, and I'm going to take you back in time.

All those years ago, we didn't have a Tilly room, just an old wooden shed that ran along the back of the house.

Lou kept her dolls pram and other toys in there. When my family went out, I had to stay in the shed, because I was too little to go out on my own. So……**I got bored**. One morning, I found a tiny, weenie hole in the wall of the house. It was just big enough for me to squeeze into.

This is difficult for you to imagine, so one of my illustrators, has drawn a special picture for you.

Look at it carefully. I found myself climbing upwards in a dirty, dark space between two walls. Now cats cannot go backwards in confined spaces, so I had to keep going forwards, and that meant upwards and onwards. I was frightened because the long climb seemed to go on forever.

Eventually, I crawled through another hole and found myself in a filthy, dirty old room, with cobwebs, water pipes and a big tank thing. Have you guessed where I was? Yes, that's right. I'd climbed up the inside of the wall (people call it a cavity wall), right up into the loft, in the roof of our house. Impressive, or what?

I was jumping around when I came across a gigantic green and red dragon, called Owen Jones. I know now that he was an old toy, but as a little kitten-baby, I thought he was real. By this time I was petrified.

Meanwhile, Mum was the first to discover I was missing from the shed. By the time Dad arrived, she was panic-stricken. She was shouting, "TC's missing. I can't find him anywhere."

"He can't be, Jill, there's no way he can get out. Perhaps he ran past you into the house."

They looked everywhere, and I could hear them upstairs, calling, "TC! TC!"

I did a "mieuw, mieuw". Only tiny sounds. That's all I could manage, but, luckily, Mum heard me.

"Julian, I know this is going to sound ridiculous, but I'm sure I heard a little meow coming from the loft."

"Mieuw, mieuw," I did it again, and this time Dad heard it.

I was sat on the floor, in the roof, when suddenly there was a rumble, and Dad came up through the floor! It was all too much for a little kitten-baby.

Of course, because I was in the loft, Dad had to open a trapdoor, pull down the ladder, climb up into the roof and rescue me.

I was a nervous blob of ginger fur when Dad grabbed me and carried me back down the ladder to safety. They made a big fuss of me, told all their friends, and Lou was speechless!

"This really happened, you know, Chris."
"Yes, TC, it's incredible you didn't get stuck."

Now you're all here, everybody, can you stay for a bit longer?

It's my birthday, and I bet you've never been to a cat's party before. Well, you've been invited to one now.........

Come to TC's Party!

As you can see, I've been sent some birthday cards.

"Wow, TC, these cards are awesome!"

"I know, Chris. They are superb.

There are beautiful pictures of me, all drawn by my children-peoples. They are the tops and they must have put a lot of work into them."

I love them all, because everyone is different. If you look closely at all the photographs you can see me as………

TC – Supercat.

Me coming out of a birthday cake – the green card behind me.

Me, as a footballer – clue, under the yellow sun.
In fact, they're all my favourites.

"Look, I've had a present too. Lou gave me this green balloon. It's bright and shiny, and I love the shape."

"It's mega, TC."

"It is, Chris. I love being Lou's pet cat."

"Now, Chris, enough chattering, and let's get this party started!" Ready, everyone?
Good, then bring it on,
and let's party!

"TC, I'd like to kick the party off by singing the birthday song. I've been practising for ages."

Chris sat up, and his little whiskers twitched with excitement. He cleared his throat, "Umph. Umph ha!", and sang at the top of his squeaky little voice,
"You to birthday happy, you to birthday ha….."

"Chris, stop! Stop!!"

"Why, TC? Everyone sings the birthday song, no matter how old they are."

"Yes, Chris, but not **backwards!**"

The little mouse looked crestfallen and dejected.

"Cheer up, Chris, everyone joining our party will help you sing, whether they're reading this on their own, or in a group, won't you? Ready, after three. 1, 2, 3.."

**Happy birthday to you, Happy birthday to you.
Happy birthday, dear TC, Happy birthday to you.**

Wow, thank you, that was outstanding. Now, let's party on! Chris and I have planned two games for you to play with us.

Can you see a letter on my forehead? That's right, it's the letter 'M'. You have to guess what word my letter M stands for.

"I know, I know, TC."

"No you don't, Chris."

"I do, I do. Please let me have a go, TC."

Oh, children-peoples, do you mind if Chris has the first turn? Well, this should be interesting.

Chris Mouse was bursting with pride.

"TC, your M stands for…….MOUSE!"

"MOUSE! You have got to be joking. Of course it doesn't stand for mouse, I'm an important cat. Now, be quiet Chris, and let's hear the children-people's ideas."

Can you make a list?

A "Guess" page, just for you.

Make your own list of "M" words:

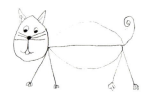

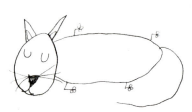

How many words have you thought of? Marvellous. Good word, but not right. What else do I hear? Magical, marmalade, musical. All terrific words, but not the right one.

"I've got it, TC. Mister Mess Maker. Your Mum is always complaining about the mess you make in the Tilly room. Loose fur, dirty paw prints, fur-balls, and spilling your food all over the floor."

"I quite like that, Chris. It's a good title, because that's what cats do."

But my M stands for…wait for it…………..

If you got it right, well done, but you're all winners for thinking of some great M words.

Now it's time for Chris's game. It's called 'Spot Chris Mouse'. Can you find Chris hiding in the following eight photographs? Look carefully, some are easy, and some are more difficult!

Number 1.

Number 2.

Number 3.

Number 4.

Number 5.

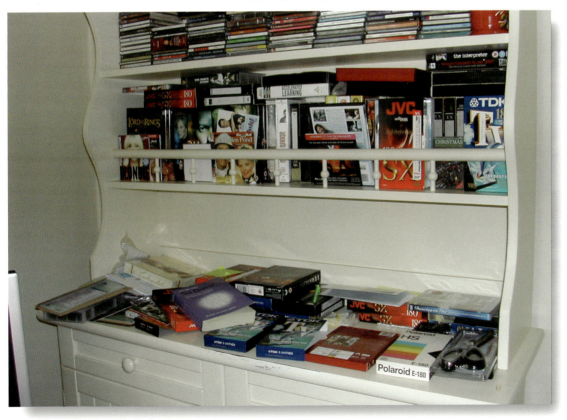

Number 6.

Number 7.

Number 8.

Did you spot him in:

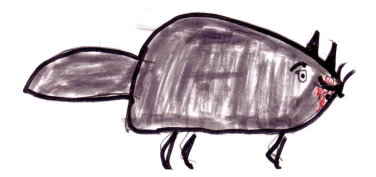

1. Perched on top of the black torch on the wall?
2. Between the plums, behind the orange?
3. Peeping out of bag of raisins (next to purple cereal box)?
4. Looking out over grey remote control?
5. Hiding in the green glove, on the white tin with the orange lid?
6. Under the red video case on the first shelf of the unit?
7. On the ground, near white petals, by the Magnolia tree?
8. By the bluebell on the rockery (see arrow below)?

Chris thought he did a good job there. Hope you enjoyed the game as much as he did!

Well, we must go now, because Chris is taking me for an animal night out……**bushing**, to celebrate my birthday.

Cats love to go out at night, but it will take lots of energy, so first it's snooze time.

Remember at the beginning of the book, I promised to tell you how I came to be called TC? Well, TC stands for one of the following. Only one answer is right.

1. **Tremendous Creature**
2. **Troublesome Cat**
3. **Terrifically Clever**
4. **Tangerine Chutney**
5. **Totally Confused**
6. **Tantalising Creation**
7. **Timid Cat**
8. **Tank Commander**
9. **Terribly Clumsy**
10. **Tom Cat**
11. **Theatrical Cat**

Turn over the page, to see if you guessed correctly, and find out how I got my name.

TC stands for....Wait for it.....**Totally Confused!!!**

I can hear you thinking, "Why would anyone call a little kitten, 'Totally Confused'?" Well may you ask.

When I came to live with my family, I was a kitten-baby. Lou wanted a little girl kitten, and so she called me "Annabella"!

(THIS IS TRUE!)

A few weeks later, Dad discovered I was a boy, and he said, jokingly, "This little kitten must be totally confused. A boy with a girl's name." Trouble was the name, 'Totally Confused' stuck, and they soon shortened it to **TC.**

I want to make one thing clear, I always knew I was a boy. But people get funny ideas, and my official name became, TC. So here I am. Did any of you get it right? Bet you didn't.

Thank you, children-peoples, for joining me today. I've had a real mint birthday. When it's your special day, I hope you have a very happy birthday. Take care of each other, and come and see me again soon.

PS. If your pet has a birthday, and you don't have much pocket money, here are a few ideas for some original presents. I love them all!

1. A small piece of scrunched up tin foil makes a smashing ball. I love chasing it around the floor, and pawing it around.

2. An old washing basket (with holes to look through). Works a treat.

3. A pet pampering day in your own home.

BUT, remember the most important thing of all, a loved pet is a happy pet!

One last game for you! There is a page of stick cats at the beginning of the book (Page 11), drawn by my children-peoples. Can you find which cat appears twice?

Have fun.

Love, TC

Answer to stick cat game on page 45.

Georgie, with children at Mama Laadi's Foster Home, 2006

Georgie Cohen, the founder and director of AfriKids, visited Northern Ghana as a student. Captivated by the smiling children, she started by decorating a Babies' Home. Today, AfriKids is sustaining ten projects in Ghana.

Georgie shows us how one person can make a difference to the world, and that is what our project of "Meet TC" is all about.

All proceeds from this book will be donated to AfriKids' Mango Tree project, and we hope it will help Mama Laadi (one of the remarkable people mentioned on the opposite page) empower the children she is caring for at her Foster Home.

AfriKids is a grass-roots charity, which works alongside communities in isolated rural areas in Northern Ghana, to help them make life better and safer for their children.

Our main aim is to enable these local communities to give their children back the right to a childhood. AfriKids' work tackles the immediate problems excluded children face, i.e. their basic need for food and water, shelter, medical care and schooling.

At the core of every AfriKids' programme are local individuals, who have dedicated their lives to making life better for children. AfriKids identifies these remarkable people, and helps them build effective, appropriate and sustainable initiatives, enabling them to reach out to hundreds more children.

Our philosophy is to:

Listen to what the community knows it needs

Empower them to make the necessary changes themselves

Ensure absolute sustainability

www.afrikids.org